LET'S-READ-AND-FIND-OUT SCIENCE®

STAGE 1

Starfish

by Edith Thacher Hurd • illustrated by Robin Brickman

HarperCollinsPublishers

For Anna Eileen Brickman,
who loves the ocean and books
–R.B.

Special thanks to Jane Tucker of the Marine Biological
Laboratory for her time and expert review.

The *Let's-Read-and-Find-Out Science* book series was originated by Dr. Franklyn M. Branley, Astronomer Emeritus and former Chairman of the American Museum–Hayden Planetarium, and was formerly co-edited by him and Dr. Roma Gans, Professor Emeritus of Childhood Education, Teachers College, Columbia University. Text and illustrations for each of the books in the series are checked for accuracy by an expert in the relevant field. For more information about Let's-Read-and-Find-Out Science books, write to HarperCollins Children's Books, 10 East 53rd Street, New York, NY 10022, or visit our Web site at http://www.harperchildrens.com.

HarperCollins®, ☞®, and Let's-Read-and-Find-Out Science® are trademarks of HarperCollins Publishers Inc.

Library of Congress Cataloging-in-Publication Data
Hurd, Edith Thacher.
    Starfish / by Edith Thacher Hurd ; illustrated by Robin Brickman.
        p.   cm. – (Let's-read-and-find-out. Stage 1)
    Originally published: Starfish. New York ; Crowell, 1962.
    Summary: A simple introduction to the appearance, growth, habits, and behavior of starfish.
    ISBN 0-06-028356-4. – ISBN 0-06-028357-2 (lib. bdg.). – ISBN 0-06-445198-4 (pbk.)
    1. Starfishes–Juvenile literature.   [1. Starfishes.]   I. Brickman, Robin, ill.   II. Hurd, Edith Thacher. Starfish.   III.
Title.   IV. Series.
QL384.A8H855   2000   99-21063
593.9'3–dc21   CIP
                                                                                                                                    AC

Typography by Elynn Cohen
1   2   3   4   5   6   7   8   9   10
❖

Starfish

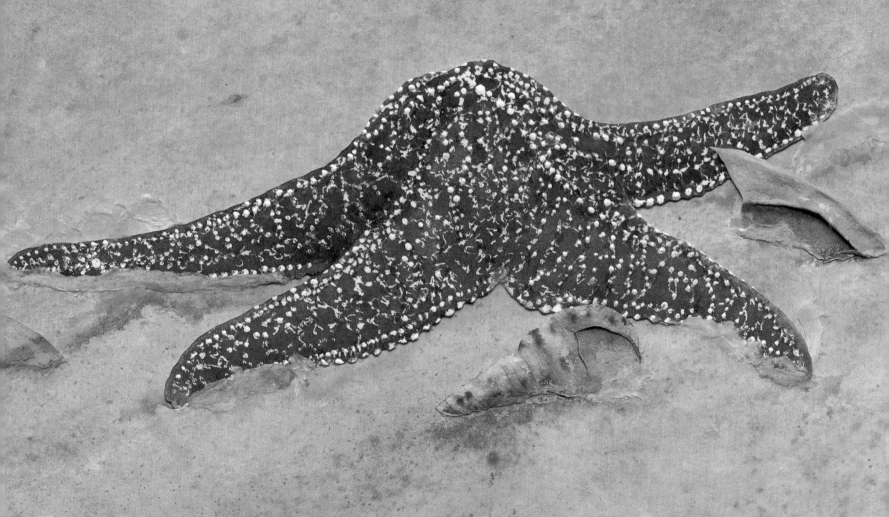

Starfish live in the sea.
Starfish live deep down in the sea.
Starfish live in pools by the sea.

5

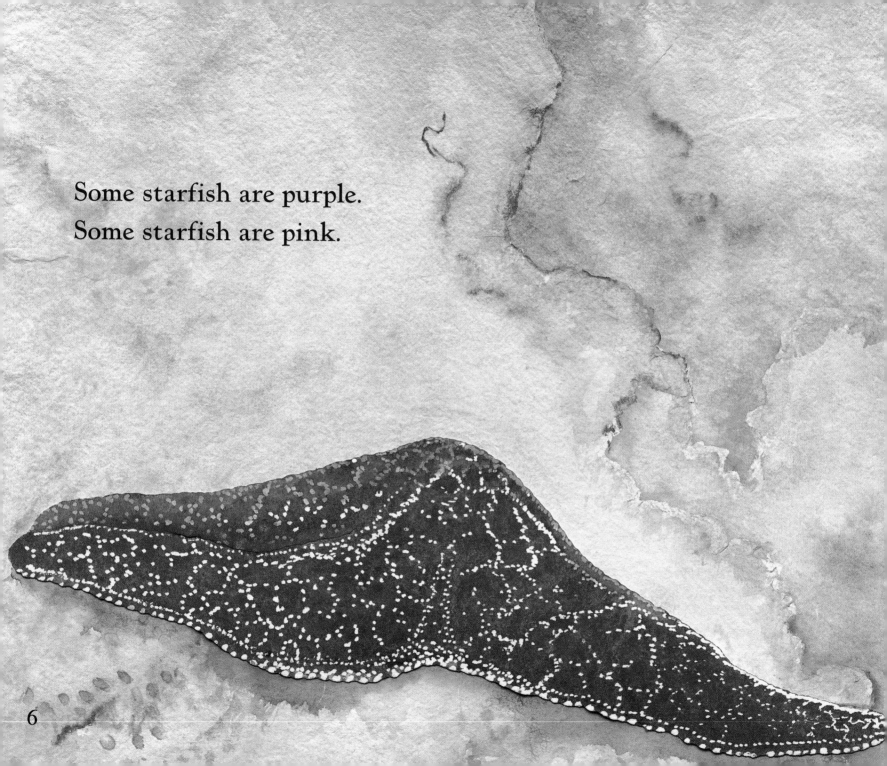

Some starfish are purple.
Some starfish are pink.

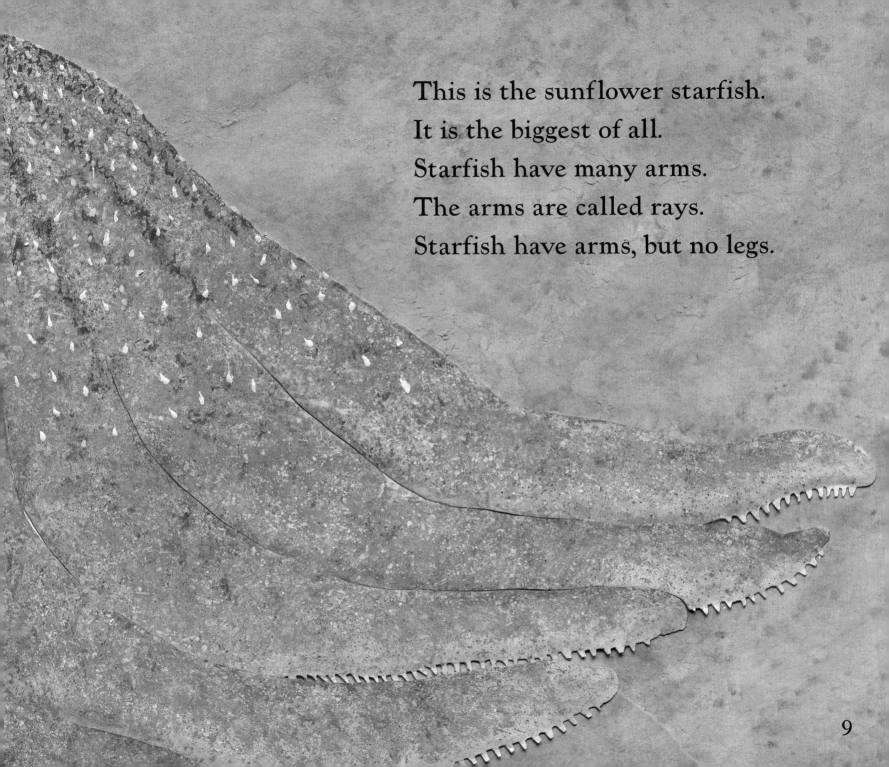

This is the sunflower starfish.
It is the biggest of all.
Starfish have many arms.
The arms are called rays.
Starfish have arms, but no legs.

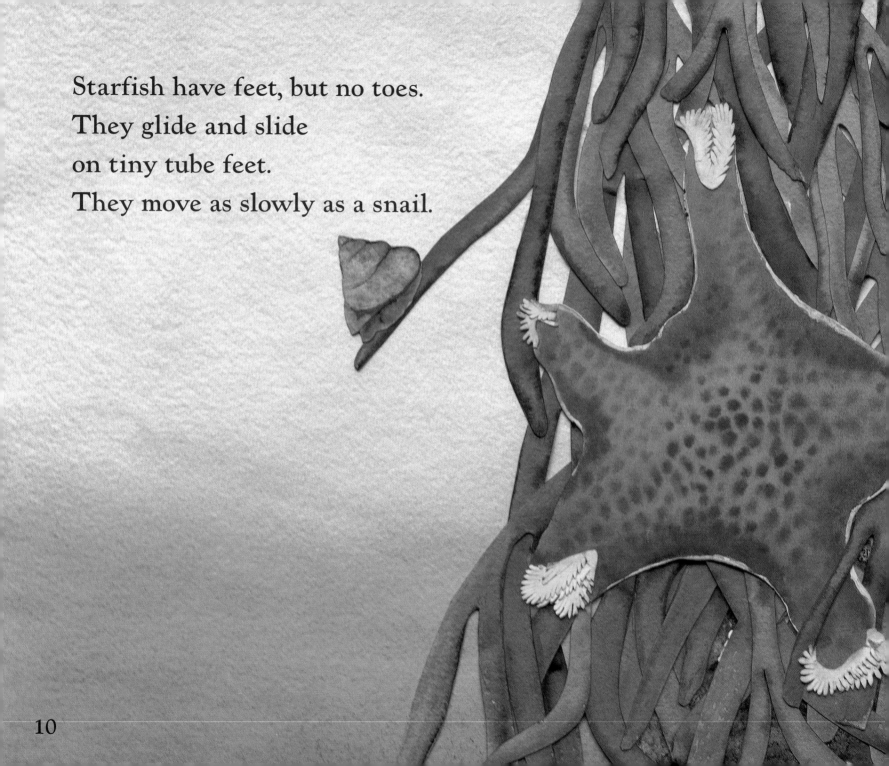

Starfish have feet, but no toes.
They glide and slide
on tiny tube feet.
They move as slowly as a snail.

11

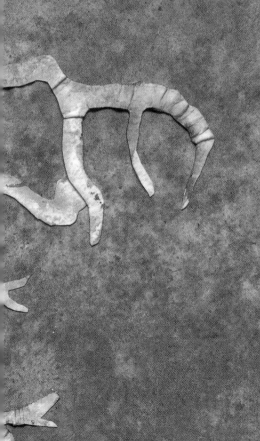

The basket star looks like a starfish,
but it is a little different.
It doesn't have tube feet.
It moves with its rays.
It has rays that go up
and rays that go down.

Tiny brittle stars are like the basket star.
They hide under rocks
in pools by the sea.

The mud star hides in the mud.
It is a starfish.
It has tiny tube feet.

A starfish has no eyes.
A starfish has no ears or nose.
Its tiny mouth is on its underside.
When a starfish is hungry,
it slides and it glides
on its tiny tube feet.

It hunts for mussels and oysters
and clams.
It feels for the mussels.
It feels for the oysters.
It feels for the clams.
It feels for something to eat.

17

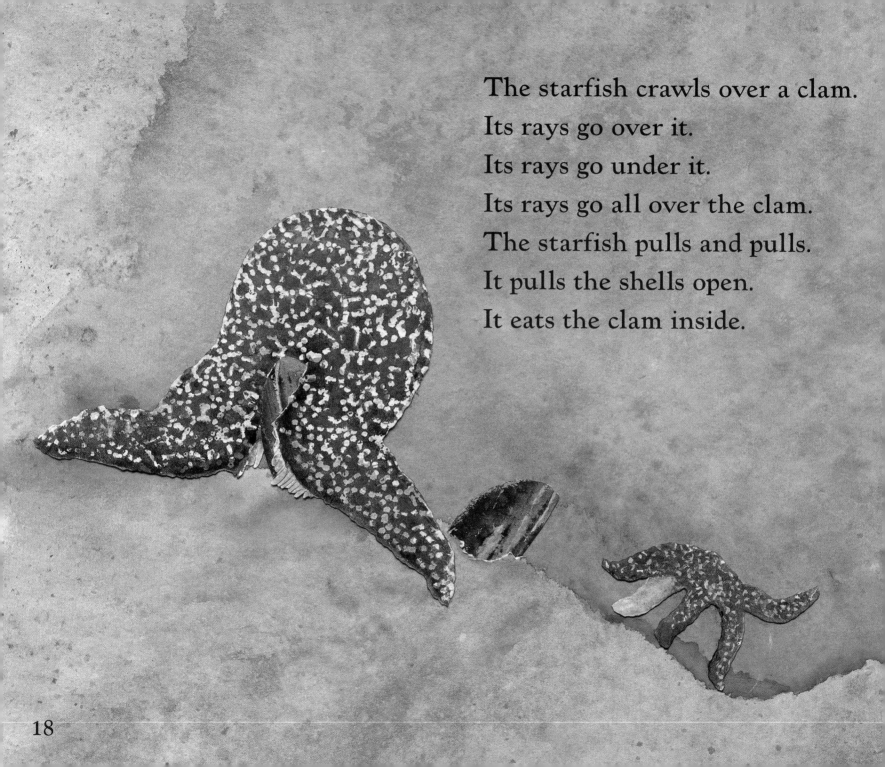

The starfish crawls over a clam.

Its rays go over it.

Its rays go under it.

Its rays go all over the clam.

The starfish pulls and pulls.

It pulls the shells open.

It eats the clam inside.

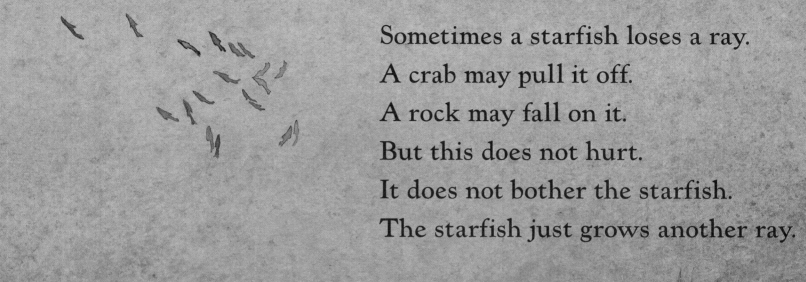

Sometimes a starfish loses a ray.
A crab may pull it off.
A rock may fall on it.
But this does not hurt.
It does not bother the starfish.
The starfish just grows another ray.

In the spring when the sun shines warm,
and the sea grows warm,
starfish lay eggs.
Starfish lay eggs in the water.
They lay many, many, many tiny eggs.
The eggs look like sand
in the sea.
The tiny eggs float in the water.
They float up and down.
They move with the waves and the tide,
up and down,
up and down.

The tiny eggs change and grow.
They float in the water.
They move with the waves,
back and forth,
back and forth.
Then they sink to the bottom
and they grow into tiny starfish.
The tiny starfish grow scratchy and hard.
They grow little rays.
They grow tiny tube feet
to crawl on.

Baby starfish eat and eat
and EAT.
First they eat tiny things
that float in the sea.
Then they eat mussels and oysters and clams.
They eat and they eat.
They grow and they grow.

26

There are many different starfish.
Some are fat.
Some are thin.
Some are prickly.
Some are prickly and pink.
Some are prickly and gray.
Some are just a tangle.

Look on the rocks
by the sea.
Look in the pools
by the sea.

Look for starfish,
the stars
of the sea. . . .

31

FIND OUT MORE ABOUT STARFISH

Starfish are not really fish. They are related to sea urchins and sand dollars. Scientists call starfish "sea stars."

• **Make your own starfish**

You will need:

pencil	sandpaper
paper	newspaper
safety scissors	paint

1. Draw or trace a starfish on the piece of paper. You can copy a starfish shape out of this book, or just draw a star like this:

2. Carefully cut out your starfish pattern.

3. Put a piece of sandpaper with the rough side down on top of a newspaper. Put your starfish pattern on the smooth side of the sandpaper and trace around it.

4. Carefully cut out your starfish.

5. Paint your starfish whatever color you wish. Be sure to keep the starfish and the paint on a sheet of newspaper as you work.

Now you have your very own starfish!

Starfish come in many different shapes and sizes. Try making different starfish shapes and using different colors of paint. If you make several starfish, you can glue them to a large sheet of paper to make a collage of your own sea of starfish.

• Find starfish

Go to the beach and have an adult help you look for starfish. Starfish are commonly found in tide pools or very shallow water. How many different shapes, sizes, and colors of starfish can you find?

Starfish are safe to touch. You can pick up a starfish gently and look on its underside for tube feet and its tiny mouth.

Remember, starfish cannot live in fresh water or on land. When you have finished looking at a starfish, be sure to put it back into the ocean.

You can also see starfish at an aquarium. If you are patient and watch very carefully, you may be able to see one slowly glide from one place to another.

• Help starfish

Starfish are among the ocean life that Greenpeace helps to preserve. Greenpeace works to protect the environment by peaceful means. To learn more about Greenpeace or to become a member, visit its web site at www.greenpeace.org or call (800) 326–0959.

• You can learn more about starfish and other sea creatures in these great books:

Seashells, Crabs and Sea Stars by Christine Kump Tibbitts,
   illustrated by Linda Garrow

My Visit to the Aquarium by Aliki

Life in a Tide Pool by Allan Fowler

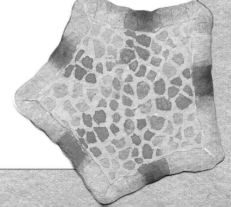